It's Easy To Play Latin.

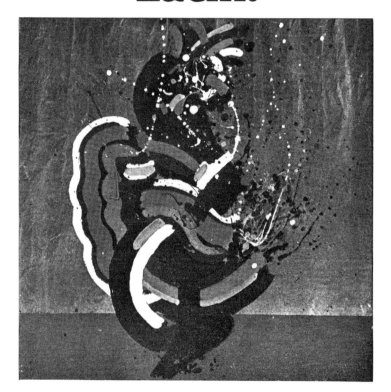

This album © Copyright 1977
Wise Publications
London/New York/Sydney/Cologne

Exclusive distributors:
Music Sales Limited
78 Newman Street, London W1P 3LA, England.
Music Sales Pty. Limited
27 Clarendon Street, Artarmon, Sydney, NSW 2064, Australia.
Music Sales Corporation
24 East 22nd Street, New York, N.Y. 10010, USA.

Music Sales complete catalogue lists thousands
of titles and is free from your local music
book shop, or direct from Music Sales Limited.
Please send 25p in stamps for postage to
Music Sales Limited, 78 Newman Street, London W1P 3LA.

Printed in England by
West Central Printing Co. Limited, London and Suffolk.

— Rumba
— Samba
— Mambo
— Cha Cha Cha

Hear CD (82) Latin Jazz

Always In My Heart 8
Amor 10 *— Beguine*
Be Mine Tonight 43
Brazil 6   *Samba   CD 82/14*
Come Closer To Me (Acércate Más) 12
Desafinado 34 *Bossa Nova CD 82/2*
                    Samba
Eso Beso 46
Fly Me To The Moon 32 *— could be Waltz*
Granada 17
Love Me With All Of Your Heart 24
Maria Elena 20 *— Waltz*
Non Dimenticar 22
Patricia 14
Perhaps, Perhaps, Perhaps 4
Perfidia 26
Sway 28
Tico Tico 40 *———— Samba*
Wave 37 *Bossa nova*
You Belong To My Heart 30

To add

in Jazz Tunes book

(Pg)
{ Girl from Ipanema 123
{ Quiet Nyht of Quiet Stars 107 A. Carlos Jobim
{ One Note Samba 93 " " "

Water Melon Man

Paso Doble

Perhaps, Perhaps, Perhaps

English Lyric by Joe Davis
Music by Osvaldo Farres

You won't ad-mit you love me,___ and so, How am I

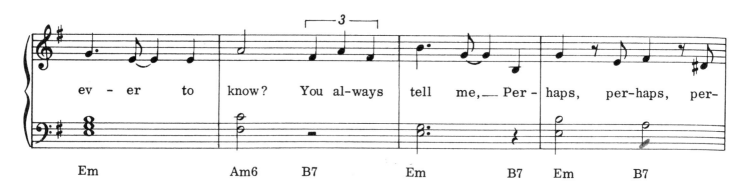

ev - er to know? You al-ways tell me,___ Per - haps, per-haps, per-

- haps.___ A mil - lion times I've asked you,___ and then I ask you

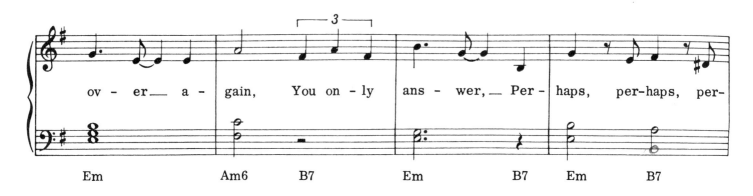

ov - er___ a - gain, You on - ly ans - wer,___ Per - haps, per-haps, per-

Brazil

Lyric by S.K. Russell
Music by Ary Barroso

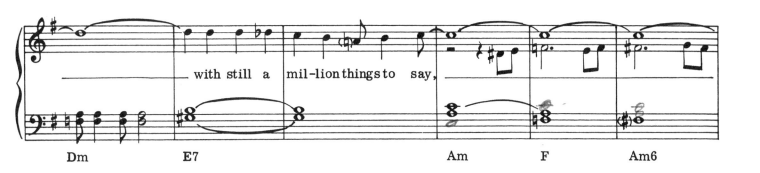

with still a mil-lion things to say,

Dm   E7   Am   F   Am6

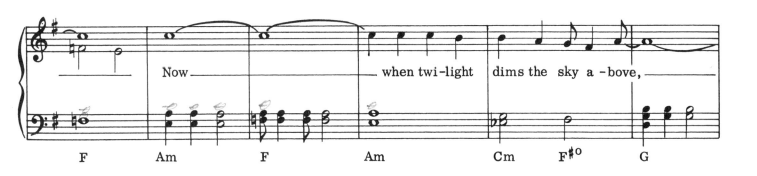

Now   when twi-light dims the sky a-bove,

F   Am   F   Am   Cm   F#o   G

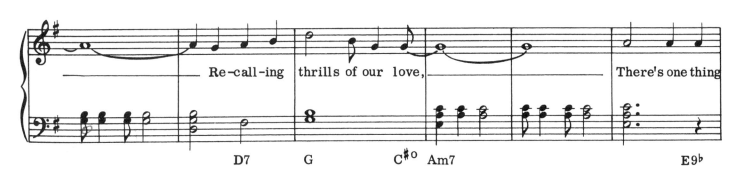

Re-call-ing thrills of our love,   There's one thing

D7   G   C#o Am7   E9♭

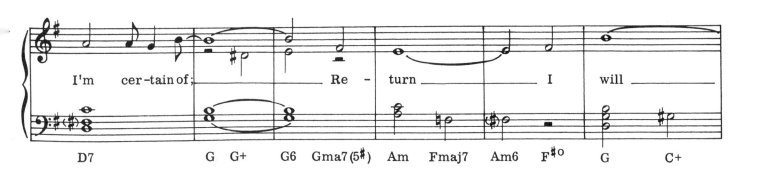

I'm cer-tain of;   Re - turn   I will

D7   G   G+   G6   Gma7(5#)   Am   Fmaj7   Am6   F#o   G   C+

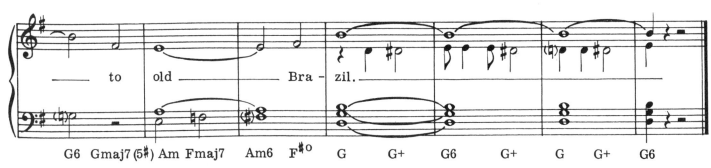

to old   Bra - zil.

G6   Gmaj7(5#)   Am   Fmaj7   Am6   F#o   G   G+   G6   G+   G   G+   G6

Always In My Heart

Lyric by Kim Gannon
Music by Ernesto Lecuona

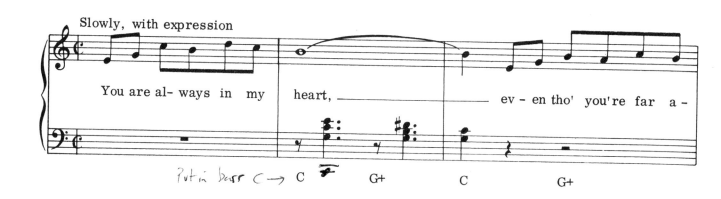

You are al- ways in my heart, even tho' you're far a-

-way, I can hear the mus- ic of the song of

love I sang with you. You are al- ways in my

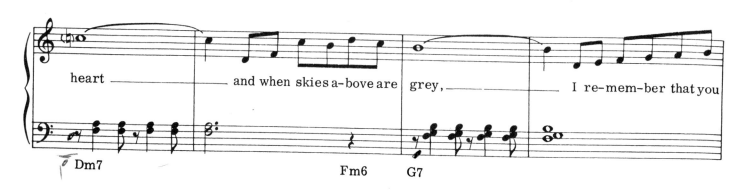

heart and when skies a-bove are grey, I re-mem-ber that you

Amor

English Lyric by Sunny Skylar
Music by Gabriel Ruiz

sounds quite so dear,   as   this soft car-ess-ing word I   know.   A - mor,   A -

Am   D7   G7   Dm7   G7   C

- mor,   my   love, _____   When you're a - way   there is no day, and nights are

lone - ly, _____   A - mor,   A - mor,   my   love,

G7   Dm

Make life di - vine,   say you'll be mine,   and love me on - ly. _____   A -

G7   C6   Ab7

- mor, _____   A - mor. _____

C6   Ab7   C

Come Closer To Me

English Lyric by Al Stewart
Music by Osvaldo Farres

Patricia

Words by Bob Marcus
Music by Peres Prado

Granada

English Words by Dorothy Dodd
Music by Agustín Lara

Maria Elena

English Lyric by S.K. Russell
Music by Lorenzo Barcelata

21

Non Dimenticar

English Lyric by Shelley Dobbins
Music by P.G. Redi

Love Me With All Of Your Heart

English Lyric by Michael Vaughn
Music by Carlos Rigual and Carlos Martinoli

Perfidia

English Lyric by Milton Leeds
Music by Alberto Dominguez

Moderato
Con espressione

To you _____ my heart cries out "Per - fid - i - a", _____

C   Am   Dm7   G7   C   Am

_____ For I found you, the love of my life, in some-bo-dy el-se's arms. _____

Dm   G7   C   Am   Dm7   F7-5   E7

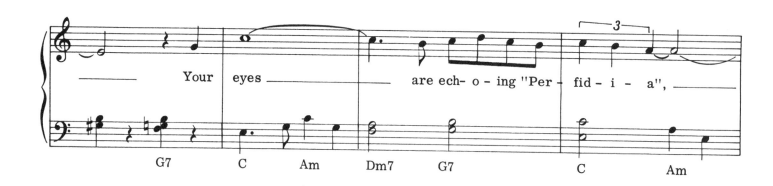

_____ Your eyes _____ are ech- o - ing "Per - fid - i - a", _____

G7   C   Am   Dm7   G7   C   Am

_____ For-get- ful of our pro-mise of love, you're shar-ing an-oth-er's charms. _____

Dm   G7   C   Am   Dm7   F7-5   E7

With a sad la-ment, my dreams have fa-ded like a bro-ken mel-o-

Dm6

-dy; While the Gods of love look down and laugh at

E7　　　　　　　　　　　　　　Dm6

what ro-man-tic fools we mor-tals be. And

E　　　　　　Dm7　Fm6　G7

now I know my love was not for you, And so I'll take it

C　Am　Dm7　G7　　　C　Am　Dm　G7

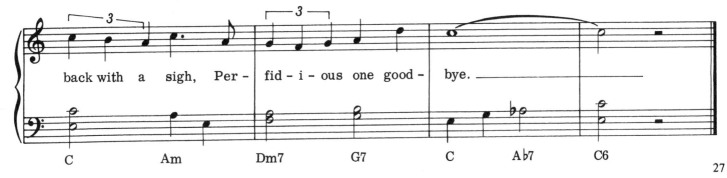

back with a sigh, Per-fid-i-ous one good-bye.

C　Am　Dm7　G7　　C　Ab7　C6

Sway

English Lyric by Norman Gimbel
Music by Pablo Beltran Ruiz

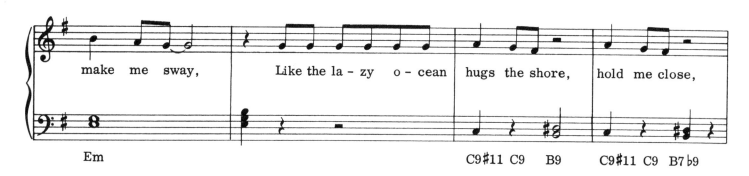

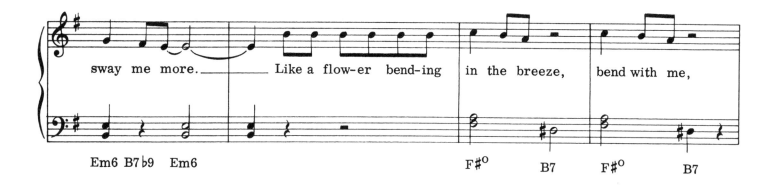

You Belong To My Heart

English Lyric by Ray Gilbert
Music by Agustín Lara

Moderately

You be - long to my heart, _____ now and for - ev - er, _____

C7   F   C6   F6   F#°   C7

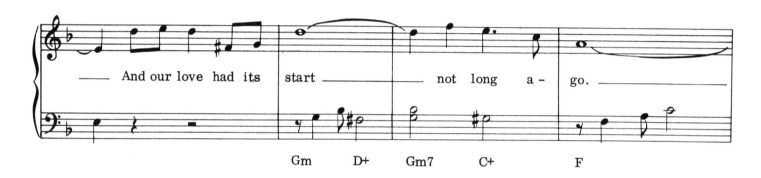

_____ And our love had its start _____ not long a - go. _____

Gm   D+   Gm7   C+   F

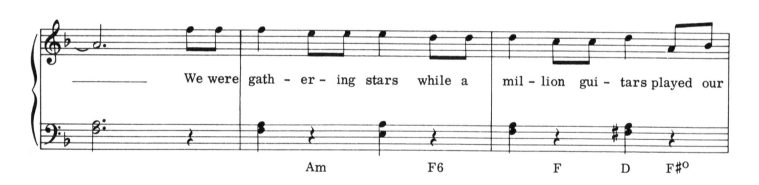

_____ We were gath - er - ing stars while a mil - lion gui - tars played our

Am   F6   F   D   F#°

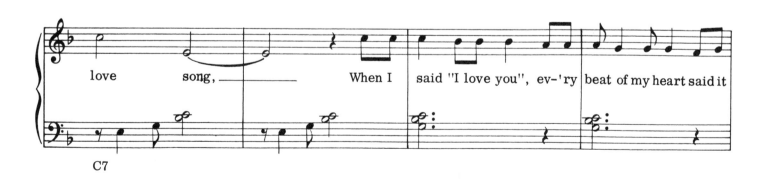

love song, _____ When I said "I love you", ev-'ry beat of my heart said it

C7

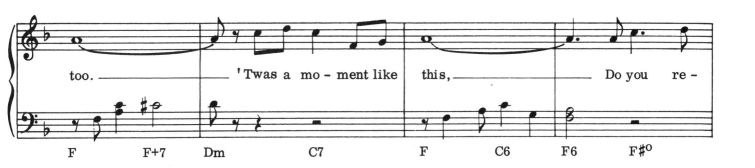

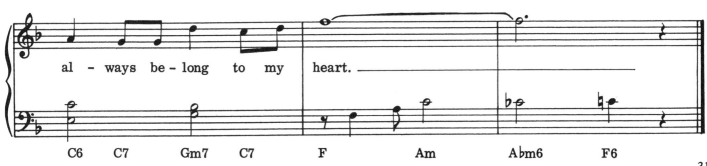

Fly Me To The Moon

Words and Music by Bart Howard

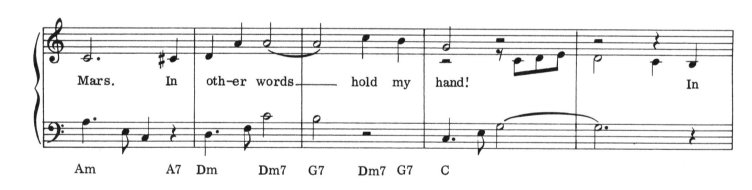

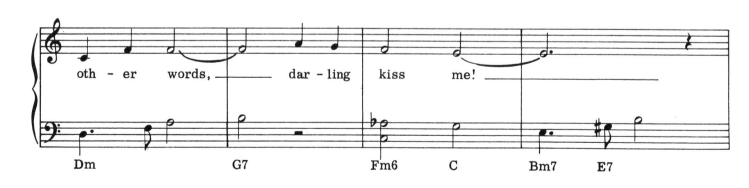

33

Desafinado

by A.C. Jobim

Wave

Words and music by Antonio Carlos Jobim

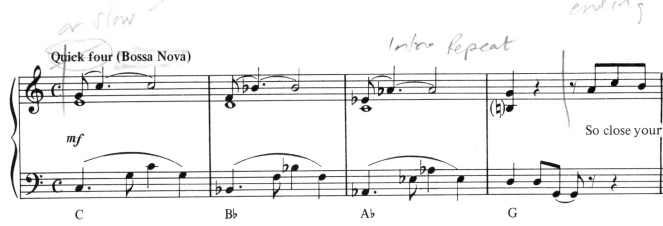

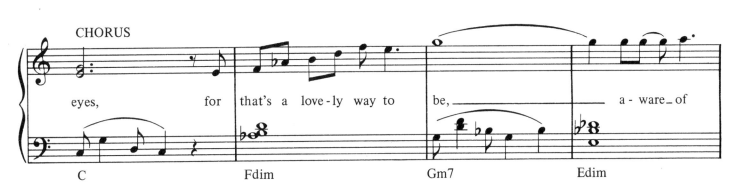

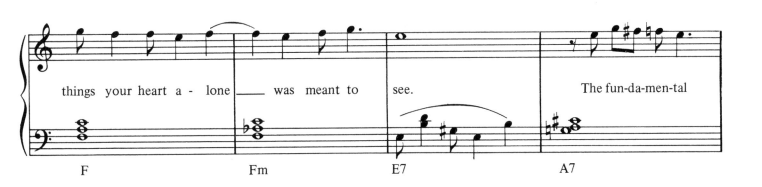

You can't de-ny, don't try to fight the ri-sing sea; ___ don't fight ___ the moon, the stars a-bove ___ and don't fight me. The fun-da-men-tal lone-li-ness goes when-ev-er two can dream a dream to-geth-er. ___ When I saw you first, the time was half past three. ___ When ___ your eyes met mine, it was e-

Cm F C Fdim Gm7

Edim F Fm E7

A7 Am7 D7 Ab7 G7

Cm F Cm F Fm Bb9

Gm7 Ebm7 Ebm6

-ter -ni-ty._____ By now we know the wave is on its way to
Fm **G7** **C** **Fdim**

be._____ Just catch___ the wave, don't be a-fraid___ of lov-ing
Gm7 **Edim** **F** **Fm**

me. The fun-da-men-tal lone-li-ness goes when-ev-er
E7 **A7** **Am7** **D7**

two can dream a dream to- geth-er._____
Ab7 **G7** **Cm** **F** **Cm** **F**

INTRO + B

C **Bb** C end **F**
Intro Ab G7

39

Tico Tico

English lyric by Ervin Drake
Music by Zequinha Abreu

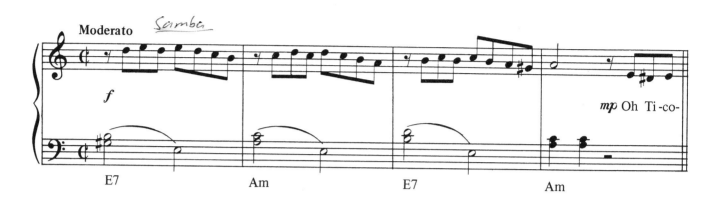

tête at eight,__ so speak, oh Ti-co, tell me is it get-ting late? If I'm on

E7   Am

time: "Cuck-oo!"__ but if I'm late, "Woo-woo!"__ The one my heart has gone to may not want to

Dm   Am   E7

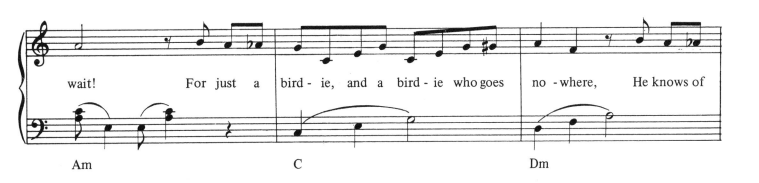

wait! For just a bird-ie, and a bird-ie who goes no-where, He knows of

Am   C   Dm

ev-'ry lov-er's lane and how to go there; For in af-fairs of the heart__ my Ti-co's

G7   C

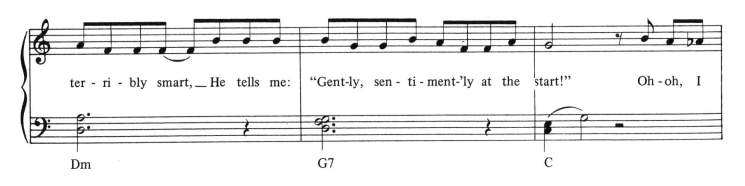

ter-ri-bly smart,__ He tells me: "Gent-ly, sen-ti-ment-'ly at the start!" Oh-oh, I

Dm   G7   C

hear my lit - tle Ti - co - Ti - co call - ing, Be - cause the time is right and shades of night are

C Dm G7

fall - ing. I love that not - so cuck-oo cuck-oo in the clock; Ti - co -

C F C

1. to Interlude |2. Fine INTERLUDE

Ti - co-Ti - co-Ti - co-Ti-co tock. tock. *sfz* *mp*

Dm G7 C C (C)

G7

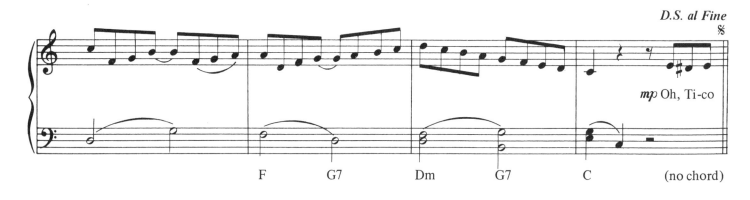

D.S. al Fine

mp Oh, Ti-co

F G7 Dm G7 C (no chord)

Be Mine Tonight

Words by Sunny Skylar
Music by Maria Teresa Lara

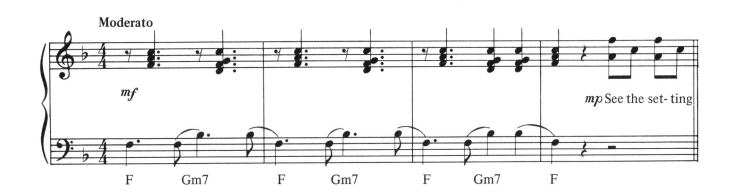

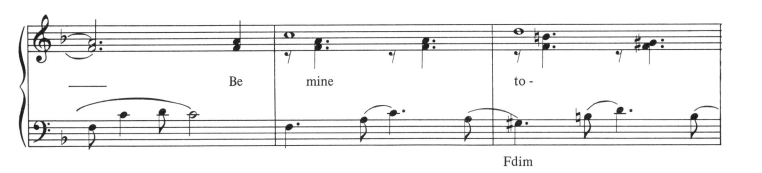

kiss I'm beg-ging you to share,_____ Be

mine_____ to - night._____

Gm   C7   F6

_____ Pro - mise this, my own, be -fore the night has flown, you'll tell me that you

care;_____ And hold

F7

me tight,_____ Whis - per

F+   B♭   F

Eso Beso

Words and music by Joe and Noel Sherman

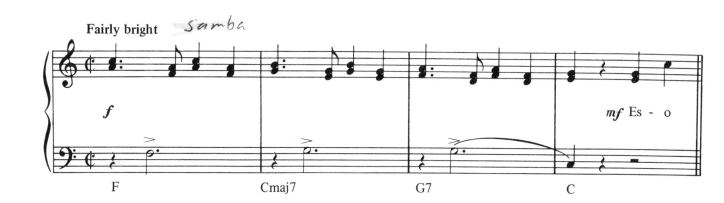

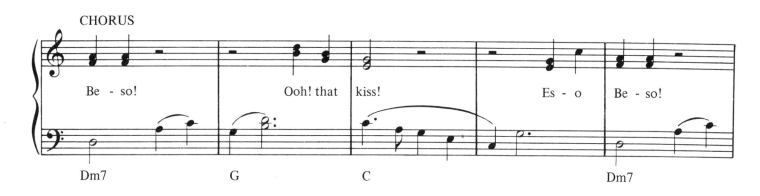

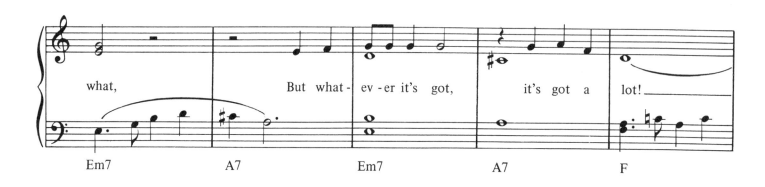

Not easy turn

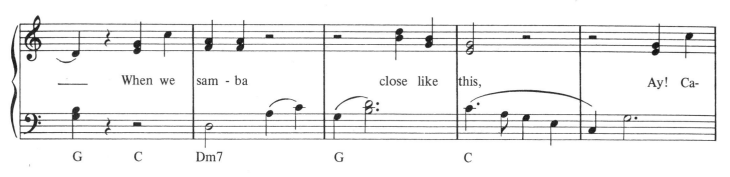

When we sam-ba close like this, Ay! Ca-

G   C   Dm7   G   C

ram - ba, Need that kiss! Hold me clo -ser

Dm7   G   C   F

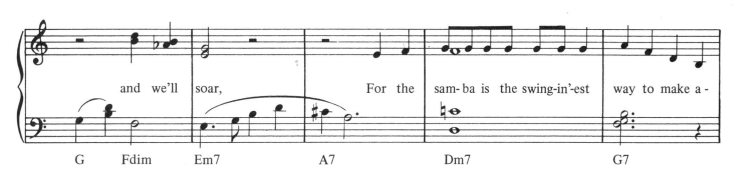

and we'll soar, For the sam-ba is the swing-in'-est way to make a-

G   Fdim   Em7   A7   Dm7   G7

EP2 T C

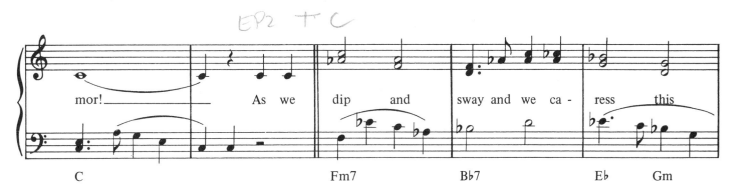

mor! As we dip and sway and we ca- ress this

C   Fm7   Bb7   Eb   Gm

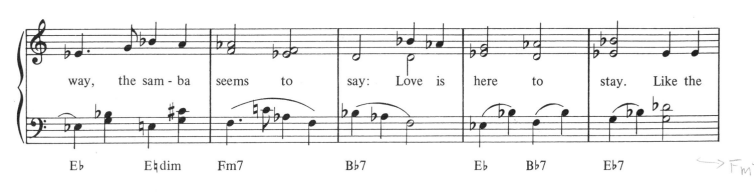

way, the sam - ba seems to say: Love is here to stay. Like the

Eb   E♮dim   Fm7   Bb7   Eb   Bb7   Eb7   →Fm7

47

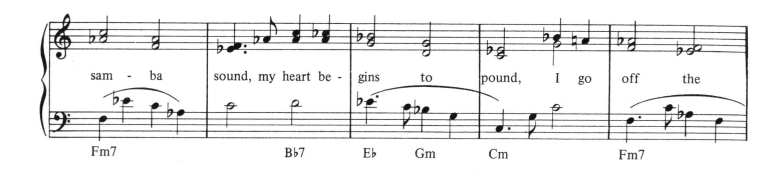

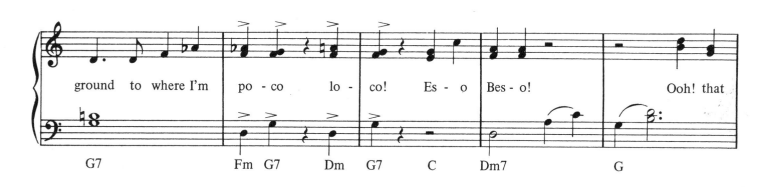

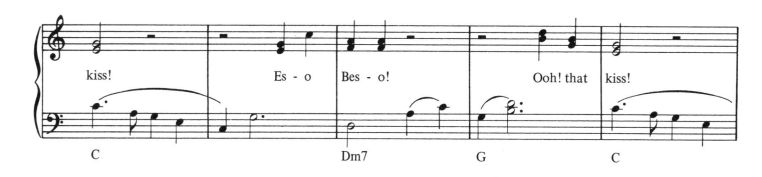

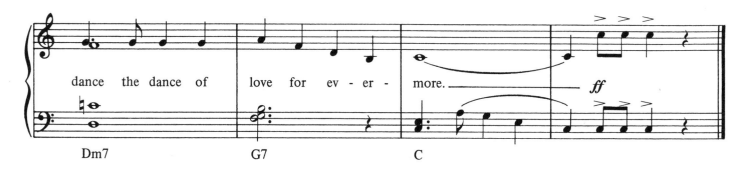

48